D0055765

$$\left[\begin{array}{c} \text{Q U O T A B L E} \\ \text{W I S D O M} \end{array}\right]$$

•

Winston Churchill

$$\begin{bmatrix} \text{Q U O T A B L E} \\ \text{W I S D O M} \end{bmatrix}$$

•

Winston Churchill

Edited by
CAROL KELLY-GANGI

FALL RIVER PRESS

New York

FALL RIVER PRESS

New York

An Imprint of Sterling Publishing
387 Park Avenue South
New York, NY 10016

FALL RIVER PRESS and the distinctive Fall River Press logo are
registered trademarks of Barnes & Noble, Inc.

Compilation © 2014 by Fall River Press
Originally published in 2013 as *The Wit and Wisdom of Winston Churchill*.

All rights reserved. No part of this publication may be reproduced, stored in a
retrieval system, or transmitted in any form or by any means (including electronic,
mechanical, photocopying, recording, or otherwise) without
prior written permission from the publisher.

The quotes in this book have been drawn from many sources, and are assumed to be accurate
as quoted in their previously published forms. Although every effort has been made to verify
the quotes and sources, the Publisher cannot guarantee their perfect accuracy.

ISBN 978-1-4549-1124-1

Distributed in Canada by Sterling Publishing
c/o Canadian Manda Group, 165 Dufferin Street
Toronto, Ontario, Canada M6K 3H6
Distributed in Australia by Capricorn Link (Australia) Pty. Ltd.
P.O. Box 704, Windsor, NSW 2756, Australia

For information about custom editions, special sales, and premium and corporate
purchases, please contact Sterling Special Sales at 800-805-5489 or
specialsales@sterlingpublishing.com.

Manufactured in the United States of America

2 4 6 8 10 9 7 5 3 1

www.sterlingpublishing.com

Image Credits
Library of Congress: 12, 18, 26, 32, 48, 54, 62, 70, 74, 86, 94, 102,
108, 114, 120, 128; Private Collection: 78, 128; U.S. Army: 2–3

CONTENTS

To my parents, Gwen and Howard, and my in-laws, Vivian and Paul,
who as children lived through the dark days of World War II
—you have my abiding love and respect.

Special thanks to Beverly Lindh and Paul Gangi for the use of
their many books written by and about Winston Churchill.

INTRODUCTION

"OF ALL THE TALENTS BESTOWED UPON MEN, NONE IS SO
PRECIOUS AS THE GIFT OF ORATORY. HE WHO ENJOYS IT
WIELDS A POWER MORE DURABLE THAN THAT OF A GREAT
KING."

When he penned these words, Winston Churchill was only twenty-three years old, a young lieutenant stationed in India. Even then, he was acutely aware of the transcendent power of words and perhaps foresaw the role that oratory would play in his own life. As a soldier, journalist, author, historian, biographer, politician, statesman, and head of state, he arguably exerted more positive influence on the world than any other single person in the twentieth century. He singularly led his country through the darkest days of World War II and bolstered both his countrymen and people around the world with words that mobilized the strength and ignited the indefatigable spirit that pushed the Allies forward to victory. A man born into and firmly entrenched in the Victorian way of life, he wielded his vast influence upon the world, both in and out of political office, for more than seventy years.

Winston Churchill: Quotable Wisdom gathers hundreds of quotations from the great leader's speeches, broadcasts, remarks, books, and other writings. In these carefully curated selections, Churchill speaks with eloquence and passion about the rising threat of Fascism in Germany, and later, of staying the course during World War II in order to preserve the world for freedom-loving peoples everywhere. There are excerpts from his most memorable war-time speeches—words that revealed Churchill's unparalleled gift for oratory and galvanized a nation.

In other selections, Churchill expresses his love of country and for the British way of life—revealing his deep-rooted and unapologetic Victorian sensibilities. His caustic wit is showcased in still other sections—especially vibrant when he was skewering his political rivals. Elsewhere, Churchill offers his inimitable wisdom on the pitfalls of political life, the real meaning of leadership, the brutal realities of war, along with a wellspring of pithy observations on such subjects as the role of a university education; the snares of the information age; the unceasing necessity of Champagne, and the questionable value of exercise and clean living.

Other sources reveal a more personal glimpse into Churchill the man. In letters, he ardently expresses his love for his wife, Clementine, and for their life together; poignantly recalls the distant awe in which he held his mother; and expresses regret at the loss of his father before realizing his dream of working together in politics. Finally, there is a selection of quotations in which writers, politicians, heads of state, historians, and members of Churchill's own family share their insights into Churchill the man, his larger-than-life personality, and his enduring legacy.

Winston Churchill: Quotable Wisdom invites readers to revisit the words of this remarkable leader who profoundly influenced the world through the course of two world wars and beyond and who will forever be remembered for his extraordinary place in history.

—Carol Kelly-Gangi

EARLY YEARS

My dear Mamma,
I hope you are quite well. I thank you very very much for the beautiful presents those Soldiers and Flags and Castle they are so nice it was so kind of you and dear Papa I send you my love and a great many kisses Your loving Winston.

—Churchill's first surviving letter, January 4, 1882
Churchill: A Life by Martin Gilbert

My mother made the same brilliant impression upon my childhood's eye. She shone for me like the Evening Star. I loved her dearly—but at a distance. My nurse was my confidante. Mrs. Everest it was who looked after me and tended all my wants. It was to her I poured out my many troubles, both now and in my schooldays.

. . . I was also miserable at the idea of being left alone among all these strangers in this great, fierce, formidable place. After all I was only seven, and I had been so happy in my nursery with all my toys. I had such wonderful toys: a real steam engine, a magic lantern, and a collection of soldiers already nearly a thousand strong. Now it was to be all lessons.

. . . How I hated this school, and what a life of anxiety I lived there for more than two years. I made very little progress at my lessons, and none at all at games. I counted the days and the hours to the end of every term, when I should return home from this hateful servitude and range my soldiers in line of battle on the nursery floor. The greatest pleasure I had in those days was reading.

. . . In retrospect these years form not only the least agreeable, but the only barren and unhappy period of my life. I was happy as a child with my toys in my nursery. I have been happier every year since I became a man. But this interlude of school makes a somber grey patch upon the chart of my journey. It was an unending spell of worries that did not then seem petty, of toil uncheered by fruition; a time of discomfort, restriction and purposeless monotony. . . . All my contemporaries and even younger boys seemed in every way better adapted to the conditions of our little world. They were far better both at the games and at the lessons. It is not pleasant to feel oneself so completely outclassed and left behind at the very beginning of the race.

—*My Early Life: A Roving Commission*

I then had one of the three or four long intimate conversations with him which are all I can boast.

—*My Early Life: A Roving Commission*, reflecting on his relationship with his father

It was, rather, from his mother that Winston derived his salient characteristics: energy, a love of adventure, ambition, a sinuous intellect, warm feelings, courage and resilience, and a huge passion for life in all its aspects.

—Paul Johnson, *Churchill*

All my dreams of comradeship with him, of entering Parliament at his side and in his support, were ended. There remained for me only to pursue his aims and vindicate his memory.

—On the death of his father in 1895, *My Early Life: A Roving Commission*

For years I thought my father with his experience and flair had discerned in me the qualities of military genius. But I was told later that he had only come to the conclusion that I was not clever enough to go to the Bar.

—*My Early Life: A Roving Commission*

She had been my dearest and most intimate friend during the whole of the twenty years I had lived.

—On the death of his nanny, Mrs. Everest, in 1895, *My Early Life: A Roving Commission*

I am getting terribly low in my finances. You say I never write for love but always for money. I think you are right but remember that you are my banker and who else have I to write to? Please send me "un peu."

—Letter to his mother, Lady Randolph Churchill, asking for some money, 1890, quoted in *The Irrepressible Churchill* compiled by Kay Halle

I realized that I must be on my best behavior—punctual, subdued, reserved—in short, display all the qualities with which I am least endowed.

> —Referring to his attendance at a dinner for the Prince of Wales, later Edward VII, *My Early Life: A Roving Commission*

Of course it is not my intention to become a mere professional soldier. I only wish to gain some experience. Some day I shall be a statesman as my father was before me.

> —Letter to Sir Felix Semon, 1896, *Churchill and the Jews: A Lifelong Friendship* by Martin Gilbert

I am 25 today—it is terrible to think how little time remains.

> —Postscript from letter to Bourke Cockran, written while Churchill was imprisoned by the Boers after the Armored Train ambush, November 30, 1899

POLITICS
AND
POLITICIANS

At Blenheim I took two very important decisions: to be born and marry. I am happily content with the decision I took on both occasions. I have never had cause to regret either.

—Remarked to a friend and first quoted in
Winston Churchill by Virginia Cowles

I have always felt that a politician is to be judged by the animosities which he excites among his opponents.

—Remarks in 1899

A politician needs the ability to foretell what is going to happen tomorrow, next week, next month, and next year. And to have the ability afterwards to explain why it didn't happen.

—Remarks in 1902

Politics are almost as exciting as war, and quite as dangerous. In war, you can only be killed once, but in politics many times.

—Remarks circa 1904

It is a very serious thing for a political creed or political party when they are compelled in spite of themselves to hail national misfortunes as a means of advancing their cause.

—Remarks in 1899

Politicians rise by toils and struggles. They expect to fall; they hope to rise again.

—Remarks in 1931

It would be a great reform in politics if wisdom could be made to spread as easily and as rapidly as folly.

—Remarks in 1947

Criticism in the body politic is like pain in the human body. It is not pleasant, but where would the body be without it?

—Remarks in 1940

It is quite flattering, but whenever I feel this way I always remember that, if instead of making a political speech, I was being hanged, the crowd would be twice as big.

—When asked if he was impressed by the crowds who gathered at his speeches, "Churchill's Rare Press Conferences," by Richard M. Langworth

The world today is ruled by harassed politicians absorbed in getting into office or turning out the other man so that not much room is left for debating great issues on their merits.

—Remarks in 1899

The dignity of a prime minister, like a lady's virtue, was not susceptible of partial diminution.

—Speech to the House of Commons, July 1905

We know that he has, more than any other man, the gift of compressing the largest amount of words into the smallest amount of thought.

—Remarks on Ramsey MacDonald's rise to prime minister

In defeat unbeatable: in victory unbearable.

—Widely attributed, about Lord Montgomery

Attlee is a very modest man. And with reason.

—Remarks on Clement Attlee, Labor Party prime minister

Occasionally he stumbled over the truth, but hastily picked himself up and hurried on as if nothing had happened.

—Remarks on Stanley Baldwin, 1936

If I valued the honorable gentleman's opinion, I might get angry.

—Remarks on a colleague, to the House of Commons, January 1913

Mr. Chamberlain loves the working man, he loves to see him work.

—Remarks on then prime minister Joseph Chamberlain, 1904

To change your mind is one thing; to turn on those who have followed your previous advice is another.

—To Lord Sydenham, August 31, 1922, after Sydenham indicated he had changed his mind about a Jewish National Home in Palestine and further stated that the Balfour Declaration in support of same had been achieved through dishonest methods

It is curious that, while in the days of my youth I was much reproached with inconsistency and being changeable, I am now scolded for adhering to the same views I had early in life and even of repeating passages from speeches which I made long before most of you were born. Of course the world moves on and we dwell in a constantly changing climate of opinion. But the broad principles and truths of wise and sane political actions do not necessarily alter with the changing moods of a democratic electorate. Not everything changes. Two and two still make four, and I could give you many other instances which go to prove that all wisdom is not new wisdom.

—Speech, Manchester, December 6, 1947

Rare and precious is the truly disinterested man.

—Remarks in 1899

At the moment, it seems quite effectively disguised.

—Response to wife Clementine's remark that his defeat in
the 1945 election "may well be a blessing in disguise"

I remember, when I was a child, being taken to the celebrated Barnum's Circus, which contained an exhibition of freaks and monstrosities, but the exhibit on the program which I most desired to see was the one described as "The Boneless Wonder." My parents judged that that spectacle would be too revolting and demoralizing for my youthful eyes, and I have waited fifty years to see the boneless wonder sitting on the Treasury Bench.

—Speech to the House of Commons, referring to
Ramsay MacDonald, January 28, 1931

Without an office, without a seat, without a party and without an appendix.

—Remarks after his defeat in 1922 when an appendectomy kept him
sidelined until just two weeks before the Parliamentary election

Anyone can rat, but it takes a certain amount of ingenuity to re-rat.

—Upon his return to the Conservative party twenty years after leaving them in 1904 for the Liberal party, circa 1924

At my time of life I have no personal ambitions, no future to provide for. And I feel I can truthfully say that I only wish to do my duty by the whole mass of the nation and of the British Empire as long as I am thought to be of use for that.

—Radio broadcast from London, March 21, 1943

GOVERNMENT
AND
DEMOCRACY

Many forms of government have been tried and will be tried in this world of sin and woe. No one pretends that democracy is perfect or all-wise. Indeed, it has been said that democracy is the worst form of government except all those other forms that have been tried from time to time.

—Speech to the House of Commons, November 11, 1947

When I am abroad, I always make it a rule never to criticize or attack the government of my own country. I make up for lost time when I come home.

—Speech to the House of Commons, April 1947

Whatever one may think about democratic government, it is just as well to have practical experience of its rough and slatternly foundations.

—Remarks in 1929

Socialism is one of the oldest and most often expounded delusions and fallacies which this world has ever been afflicted by. It consists not merely in a general leveling of mankind, but in keeping them level once they have been beaten down.

—Remarks in 1922

We want to draw a line below which we will not allow persons to live and labor, yet above which they may compete with all the strength of their manhood. We want to have free competition upwards; we decline to allow free competition downwards. We do not want to pull down the structure of science and civilization but to spread a net on the abyss.

—Speech in which Churchill contrasts Liberalism with Socialism, Glasgow, Scotland, October 1906

The inherent vice of Capitalism is the unequal sharing of blessings; the inherent virtue of Socialism is the equal sharing of miseries.

—Speech to the House of Commons, October 22, 1945

I am a child of the House of Commons. I was brought up in my father's house to believe in democracy. "Trust the people"—that was his message. . . . I owe my advancement entirely to the House of Commons, whose servant I am. In my country, as in yours, public men are proud to be the servants of the State and would be ashamed to be its masters. Therefore I have been in full harmony all my life with the tides which have flowed on both sides of the Atlantic against privilege and monopoly.

—Speech to a Joint Session of Congress, given after the Japanese attack on Pearl Harbor, December 26, 1941

I will not pretend that, if I had to choose between Communism and Nazism, I would choose Communism. I hope not to be called upon to survive in the world under a government of either of those dispensations.

—Speech to the House of Commons, April 14, 1937

If you destroy a free market you create a black market.

—Remarks in 1949

A nation without a conscience is a nation without a soul. A nation without a soul is a nation that cannot live.

—Remarks in 1951

Hatred plays the same part in government as acids in chemistry.

—Remarks in 1929

WORLD WAR II

Now the demand is that Germany should be allowed to rearm. . . . Do not let His Majesty's Government believe that all that Germany is asking for is equal status. . . . All these bands of sturdy Teutonic youths, marching through the streets and roads of Germany, with the light and desire in their eyes to suffer for their Fatherland, when they have the weapons, believe me they will ask for the return of lost territories and lost colonies.

—Speech to the House of Commons, November 23, 1932

The Government simply cannot make up their minds, or they cannot get the Prime Minister to make up his mind. So they go on in strange paradox, decided only to be undecided, resolved to be irresolute, adamant for drift, solid for fluidity, all-powerful to be impotent. So we go on preparing more months and years—precious, perhaps vital to the greatness of Britain—for the locusts to eat.

—Speech to the House of Commons, November 12, 1936

I will begin by saying what everybody would like to ignore or forget but which must nevertheless be stated, namely that we have sustained a total and unmitigated defeat, and France has suffered even more than we have. . . . the German dictator, instead of snatching the victuals from the table, has been content to have them served to him course by course.

—Speech to the House of Commons, October 5, 1938, referring to the Munich Agreement that marked the partition and demise of Czechoslovakia

My dear Churchill:

It is because you and I occupied similar positions in the World War that I want you to know how glad I am that you are back again at the Admiralty. . . . What I want you and the Prime Minister to know is that I shall at all times welcome it if you will keep me in touch personally with anything you want me to know about. You can always send sealed letters through your pouch or my pouch.

I am glad you did the Marlboro [sic] volumes before this thing started—and I much enjoyed reading them.

—Letter from President Franklin Delano Roosevelt to Churchill,
September 11, 1939, *Churchill in America 1895–1961:*
A Loving Portrait by Robert H. Pilpel

I was conscious of a profound sense of relief. At last I had authority to give directions over the whole scene. I felt as if I were walking with destiny, and that all my past life had been but a preparation for this hour and for this trial. . . . My warnings over the past six years had been so numerous, so detailed and were now so terribly vindicated, that no one could gainsay me. I could not be reproached either for making the war or with want of preparation for it. I thought I knew a good deal about it all and I was sure I would not fail.

—*The Second World War: The Gathering Storm*, vol. 1, on his
appointment to prime minister in May 1940

I would say to the House, as I said to those who have joined this Government: "I have nothing to offer but blood, toil, tears and sweat."

We have before us an ordeal of the most grievous kind. We have before us many, many long months of struggle and of suffering. You ask what is our policy? I will say: It is to wage war, by sea, land and air, with all our might and with all the strength that God can give us; to wage war against a monstrous tyranny, never surpassed in the dark, lamentable catalogue of human crime. That is our policy. You ask, What is our aim? I answer in one word: Victory—victory at all costs, victory in spite of all terror, victory, however long and hard the road may be; for without victory, there is no survival.

—First speech as prime minister, to the House of Commons, May 10, 1940

Even though large tracts of Europe and many old and famous States have fallen or may fall into the grip of the Gestapo and all the odious apparatus of Nazi rule, we shall not flag or fail. We shall go on to the end. We shall fight in France, we shall fight on the seas and oceans, we shall fight with growing confidence and growing strength in the air. We shall defend our island, whatever the cost may be. We shall fight on the beaches, we shall fight on the landing grounds, we shall fight in the fields and in the streets, we shall fight in the hills. We shall never surrender!

—Speech to the House of Commons, June 4, 1940, following
the evacuation of British and French armies from Dunkirk
as the Nazis bulldozed their way through France

What General Weygand called the Battle of France is over. I expect that the battle of Britain is about to begin. Upon this battle depends the survival of Christian civilization. Upon it depends our own British life, and the long continuity of our institutions and our Empire. The whole fury and might of the enemy must very soon be turned on us. Hitler knows that he will have to break us in this island or lose the war. If we can stand up to him, all Europe may be free and the life of the world may move forward into broad, sunlit uplands. But if we fail, then the whole world, including the United States, including all that we have known and cared for, will sink into the abyss of a new Dark Age made more sinister, and perhaps more protracted, by the lights of perverted science. Let us therefore brace ourselves to our duties, and so bear ourselves that if the British Empire and its Commonwealth last for a thousand years, men will still say, "This was their Finest Hour."

—Speech to the House of Commons, June 18, 1940,
following the collapse of France

This is no war of chieftains or of princes, of dynasties or national ambition; it is a war of peoples and of causes. There are vast numbers, not only in this island but in every land, who will render faithful service in this war but whose names will never be known, whose deeds will never be recorded. This is a war of the Unknown Warriors; but let all strive without failing in faith or in duty, and the dark curse of Hitler will be lifted from our age.

—BBC broadcast, London, July 14, 1940

The gratitude of every home in our island, in our Empire, and indeed throughout the world, except in the abodes of the guilty, goes out to the British airmen who, undaunted by odds, unwearied in their constant challenge and mortal danger, are turning the tide of the world war by their prowess and by their devotion. Never in the field of human conflict was so much owed by so many to so few.

—Speech to the House of Commons, paying tribute
to the Royal Air Force, August 20, 1940

Here is the answer which I give to President Roosevelt: Put your confidence in us. . . . We shall not fail or falter; we shall not weaken or tire. Neither the sudden shock of battle, nor the long-drawn trials of vigilance and exertion will wear us down. Give us the tools and we will finish the job.

—Radio address referring to the Lend-Lease Act, February 9, 1941

Far be it from me to paint a rosy picture of the future. Indeed, I do not think we should be justified in using any but the most somber tones and colors while our people, our Empire and indeed the whole English-speaking world are passing through a dark and deadly valley. But I should be failing in my duty if, on the other wise, I were not to convey the true impression, that a great nation is getting into its war stride.

—Speech to the House of Commons, January 22, 1941

The British nation is unique in this respect. They are the only people who like to be told how bad things are, who like to be told the worst.

—Speech to the House of Commons, June 10, 1941

So now this bloodthirsty guttersnipe must launch his mechanized armies upon new fields of slaughter, pillage and devastation.

—Radio broadcast on the night Hitler invaded Russia, June 1941. Churchill, an avowed anti-Communist, immediately pledged complete British aid to Russia

The mood of Britain is wisely and rightly averse from every form of shallow or premature exultation. This is no time for boasts or glowing prophecies, but there is this—a year ago our position looked forlorn, and well nigh desperate, to all eyes but our own. Today we may say aloud before an awe-struck world, "We are still masters of our fate. We still are captain of our souls."

—Speech to the House of Commons, September 9, 1941

This is the lesson: never give in, never give in, never, never, never, never—in nothing, great or small, large or petty—never give in except to convictions of honor and good sense. Never yield to force; never yield to the apparently overwhelming might of the enemy.

—Remarks at Harrow School, his childhood alma mater, October 29, 1941

I go about the country whenever I can escape for a few hours or for a day from my duty at headquarters, and I see the damage done by the enemy attacks; but I also see side by side with the devastation and amid the ruins quiet, confident, bright and smiling eyes, beaming with a consciousness of being associated with a cause far higher and wider than any human or personal issue. I see the spirit of an unconquerable people. I see a spirit bred in freedom, nursed in a tradition which has come down to us through the centuries, and which will surely at this moment, this turning-point in the history of the world, enable us to bear our part in such a way that none of our race who come after us will have any reason to cast reproach upon their sires.

—Speech at Bristol University, April 12, 1941

In two or three minutes Mr. Roosevelt came through. Mr. President, what's this about Japan? "It's quite true," he replied. "They have attacked us at Pearl Harbor. We are all in the same boat now."

. . . No American will think it wrong of me if I proclaim that to have the United States at our side was to me the greatest joy. I could not foretell the course of events. I do not pretend to have measured accurately the martial might of Japan, but now at this very moment I knew the United States was in the war, up to the neck and in to the death. So we had won after all! . . . Hitler's fate was sealed. Mussolini's fate was sealed. As for the Japanese, they would be ground to powder.

—The Second World War: The Grand Alliance, vol. 3

It becomes still more difficult to reconcile Japanese action with prudence or even with sanity. What kind of people do they think we are?

—Speech to Congress, December 26, 1941

When I warned them [the French Government] that Britain would fight on alone whatever they did, their generals told their Prime Minister and his divided Cabinet, "In three weeks England will have her neck wrung like a chicken." Some chicken! Some neck!

—Speech to Canadian Parliament,
December 30, 1941

Here's to a year of toil—a year of struggle and peril, and a long step forward towards victory. May we all come through safe and with honor.

—New Year's Day, 1942, on the train back from Ottawa

Then Hitler made his second grand blunder. He forgot about the winter. There is a winter, you know, in Russia. For a good many months the temperature is apt to fall very low. There is snow, there is frost, and all that. Hitler forgot about this Russian winter. He must have been very loosely educated. We all heard about it at school; but he forgot it. I have never made such a bad mistake as that. So winter came, and fell upon his ill-clad armies, and with the winter came the valiant Russian counterattacks.

—Broadcast, London, May 10, 1942

The Germans have received back again that measure of fire and steel which they have so often meted out to others. Now this is not the end. It is not even the beginning of the end. But it is, perhaps, the end of the beginning.

—Speech following the Allied victory over Gen. Rommel's army at El Alamein in North Africa, November 10, 1942

We mean to hold our own. I have not become the King's First Minister in order to preside over the liquidation of the British Empire.

—Speech at Mansion House, London, November 10, 1942

War is full of mysteries and surprises. A false step, a wrong direction, an error in strategy, discord or lassitude among the Allies, might soon give the common enemy power to confront us with new and hideous facts. We have surmounted many serious dangers, but there is one grave danger which will go along with us till the end; that danger is the undue prolongation of the war. No one can tell what new complications and perils might arise in four or five more years of war. And it is in the dragging-out of the war at enormous expense, until the democracies are tired or bored or split, that the main hopes of Germany and Japan just now reside.

—Speech to Congress, May 1943

How much easier it is to join bad companions than to shake them off!

—August 31, 1943, referring to the fall of Mussolini several weeks earlier

To achieve the extirpation of Nazi tyranny there are no lengths of violence to which we will not go.

—Speech to Parliament, September 21, 1943

On my right sat the President of the United States, on my left the Master of Russia. Together we controlled practically all the naval and three-quarters of all the air forces in the world, and could direct armies of nearly twenty millions of men, engaged in the most terrible of wars that had yet occurred in human history.

—Writing about his 1943 meeting with FDR and Stalin in Teheran, *The Second World War: Closing the Ring*, vol. 5

I have left the obvious, essential fact to this point, namely, that it is the Russian Armies who have done the main work in tearing the guts out of the German army. In the air and on the oceans we could maintain our place, but there was no force in the world which could have been called into being, except after several more years, that would have been able to maul and break the German army unless it had been subjected to the terrible slaughter and manhandling that has fallen to it through the strength of the Russian Soviet Armies.

—Speech to the House of Commons, August 2, 1944

There is no doubt that this is probably the greatest and most horrible crime ever committed in the whole history of the world, and it has been done by scientific machinery by nominally civilized men in the name of a great State and one of the leading races of Europe. It is quite clear that all concerned in this crime who may fall into our hands, including the people who only obeyed orders by carrying out the butcheries, should be put to death after their association with the murders has been proved.

—To his foreign secretary, July 11, 1944,
upon learning the truth about Auschwitz,
The Churchill Center, Inc.

No words can express the horror which is felt by His Majesty's Government and their principal Allies at the proofs of these frightful crimes now daily coming into view. . . . I have this morning received an informal message from General Eisenhower saying that the new discoveries, particularly at Weimar, far surpass anything previously exposed. He invites me to send a body of members of Parliament at once to his Headquarters in order that they may themselves have ocular and first-hand proof of these atrocities.

—Speech to the House of Commons, April 19, 1945

The decision to use the atomic bomb was taken by President Truman and myself at Potsdam, and we approved the military plans to unchain the dread, pent-up forces. . . . The Bomb brought peace, but men alone can keep that peace, and henceforward they will keep it under penalties which threaten the survival, not only of civilization but of humanity itself. I may say that I am in entire agreement with the president that the secrets of the atomic bomb should so far as possible not be imparted at the present time to any other country in the world. This is in no design or wish for arbitrary power, but for the common safety of the world. Nothing can stop the progress of research and experiment in every country, but although research will no doubt proceed in many places, the construction of the immense plants necessary to transform theory into action cannot be improvised in any country.

—Speech to the House of Commons, August 16, 1945

A small lion was walking between a huge Russian bear and a great American elephant, but perhaps it would prove to be the lion who knew the way.

—Remarked to exiled Czech President Beneš about the Yalta Conference, February 24, 1945, *Churchill: A Life* by Martin Gilbert

In war: resolution. In defeat: defiance. In victory: magnanimity. In peace: goodwill.

—*The Second World War: The Gathering Storm,* vol. I, epigraph

The Nuremburg trials are over, and the guilty leaders of the Nazi regime have been hanged by the conquerors. We are told that thousands yet remain to be tried, and that vast categories of Germans are classed as potentially guilty because of their association with the Nazi regime. After all, in a country which is handled as Germany was, the ordinary people have very little choice about what to do. I think some consideration should always be given to ordinary people. Everyone is not Pastor Nimbler or a martyr, and when ordinary people are hurled this way and that, when the cruel hands of tyrants are laid upon them and vile systems of regimentation are imposed and enforced by espionage and other forms of cruelty, there are great numbers of people who will succumb.

—Speech to the House of Commons, November 12, 1946

We must all turn our backs upon the horrors of the past. We must look to the future. We cannot afford to drag forward cross the years that are to come the hatreds and revenges which have sprung from the injuries of the past.

—Speech at Zurich University, September 19, 1946

There can hardly ever have been a war more easy to prevent than this second Armageddon. . . . Britain, France, and the United States have only to repeat the same well-meaning, short-sighted behavior towards the new problems which in singular resemblance confront us today to bring about a third convulsion from which none may live to tell the tale.

—*The Second World War: The Gathering Storm*, vol. I

On the night of 10 May 1940, at the outset of the mighty Battle of Britain, I acquired the chief power in the State, which henceforth I wielded in ever-growing measure for five years and three months of world war, at the end of which time, all our enemies having surrendered unconditionally or being about to do so, I was immediately dismissed by the British electorate from all further conduct of their affairs.

—Reflecting on his ouster from role of prime minister,
Churchill by Paul Johnson

LEADERSHIP

There is only one duty, only one safe course, and that is to try to be right and not to fear to do or say what you believe to be right. That is the only way to deserve and to win the confidence of our great people in these days of trouble.

—Remarks on September 30, 1941

Real leaders of men do not come forward offering to lead. They show the way, and when it has been found to lead to victory they accept as a matter of course the allegiance of those who have followed.

—*Lord Randolph Churchill*, vol. 2

Men and kings must be judged in the testing moments of their lives. Courage is rightly esteemed the first of human qualities because, as has been said, it is the quality which guarantees all others.

—Restatement of Samuel Johnson's quote on courage, July 1931

There is no worse mistake in public leadership than to hold out false hopes soon to be swept away. The British people can face peril or misfortune with fortitude and buoyancy, but they bitterly resent being deceived or finding that those responsible for their affairs are themselves dwelling in a fool's paradise.

—Remarks, 1951

Nobody ever launched an attack without having misgivings beforehand. You ought to have misgivings before; but when the moment of action is come, the hour of misgivings is passed. It is often not possible to go backward from a course which has been adopted in war. A man must answer "Aye" or "No" to the great questions which are put, and by that decision he must be bound.

—Speech to the House of Commons, November 15, 1915

When one has reached the summit of power and surmounted so many obstacles, there is a danger of becoming convinced that one can do anything one likes and that any strong personal view is necessarily acceptable to the nation and can be enforced upon one's subordinates.

—*The Wit and Wisdom of Winston Churchill* edited by James C. Humes

It is a fine thing to be honest; but it is very important for a Prime Minister to be right.

—Remarks, 1923

I still believe that vast and fearsome as the human scene has become, personal contacts of the right people in the right place at the right time may yet have a potent and valuable part to play in the cause of peace which is in our hearts.

—Remarks on March 14, 1955

After things are over it is easy to choose the fine mental and moral positions which one should adopt.

—Remarks, 1950

Strength is granted to us all when we are needed to serve great causes.

—Remarks, 1946

When you feel you cannot continue in your position for another minute, and all that is in human power has been done, that is the moment when the enemy is most exhausted, and when one step forward will give you the fruits of the struggle you have borne.

—Widely attributed

GREAT BRITAIN

England would gain far more from the rising tide of Tory democracy than from the dried-up drain-pipe of Radicalism.

—First political speech, given to the Conservative Primrose League
at Claverton Manor, near Bath, 1897

They are a class of right honorable Gentlemen—all good men, all honest men—who are ready to make great sacrifices for their opinions, but they have no opinions. They are ready to die for the truth, if they only knew what the truth was.

—Remarks in 1903, reflecting his increasing displeasure
with his Tory colleagues

While large numbers of persons enjoy great wealth, while the mass of the artisan classes are abreast of and in advance of their fellows in other lands, there is a minority, considerable in numbers, whose condition is a disgrace to a scientific and professedly Christian civilization, and constitutes a grave and increasing peril to the state.

—Speech addressing unemployment, 1908

We have got all we want in territory, but our claim to be left in undisputed enjoyment of vast and splendid possessions, largely acquired by war and largely maintained by force, is one which often seems less reasonable to others than to us.

—Speech to the House of Commons, March 17, 1914

The more serious physical wounds are often surprisingly endurable at the moment they are received. There is an interval of uncertain length before the sensation is renewed. The shock numbs but does not paralyze: the wound bleeds but does not smart. So it is with the great reverses and losses of life.

—Remarks after his resignation from the Admiralty after the botched
military attack on the Dardanelles, 1915, *Clementine Churchill:
The Biography of a Marriage* by Mary Soames

I thought he would die of grief.

—Clementine Churchill's words to his biographer about the Dardanelle crisis,
Clementine Churchill: The Biography of a Marriage by Mary Soames

The integrity of their quarrel is one of the few institutions that has been unaltered in the cataclysm which has swept the world. That says a lot for the persistency with which Irishmen on the one side or the other are able to pursue their controversies. It says a great deal for the power which Ireland has, both Nationalist and Orange, to lay their hands upon the vital strings of British life and politics, and to hold, dominate, and convulse, year after year, generation after generation, the politics of this powerful country.

—Speech to the House of Commons, February 16, 1922

There are two ways in which a gigantic debt may be spread over new decades and future generations. There is the right and healthy way and there is the wrong and morbid way. The wrong way is to fail to make the utmost provision for amortization which prudence allows, to aggravate the burden of the debt by fresh borrowing, to live from hand to mouth, and from year to year, and to exclaim with Louis XVI: "After me, the deluge."

—Speech to the House of Commons, April 1927

It is alarming and also nauseating to see Mr. Gandhi, a seditious Middle Temple lawyer, now posing as a fakir of a type well known in the East, striding half-naked up the steps of the viceregal palace, while he is still organizing and conducting a defiant campaign of civil disobedience, to parley on equal terms with the representative of the King-Emperor. Such a spectacle can only increase the unrest in India.

—Speech, Winchester House, Epping, February 23, 1931. The speech, fiercely critical of Gandhi, was much maligned in India and Great Britain as well

The British Lion, so fierce and valiant in bygone days, so dauntless and unconquerable through all the agony of Armageddon, can now be chased by rabbits from the fields and forest of his former glory. It is not that our strength is seriously impaired. We are suffering from a disease of the will. We are the victims of a nervous collapse, of a morbid state of mind.

—Remarks on March 5, 1931, referring to parliamentary pressure to pass the India Bill, which would be a step closer for India's complete independence

It is a curious fact about the British Islanders, who hate drill and have not been invaded for a nearly thousand years, that as danger comes nearer and grows they become progressively less nervous; when it is imminent they are fierce, when it is mortal they are fearless.

—*The Second World War: The Gathering Storm*, vol. I

In this island we have today achieved in a high degree the blessings of civilization. There is freedom; there is law; there is love of country; there is prosperity. There are unmeasured opportunities of correcting abuses and making further progress.

—Speech at University of Bristol, July 2, 1938

In Great Britain, governments often change their policies without changing their men. In France, they usually change their men without changing their policy.

—*Step by Step: 1936–1939*

I have an invincible confidence in the genius of Britain. I believe in the instinctive wisdom of our well-tried democracy. I am sure they will speak now in ringing tones, and that their decision will vindicate the hopes of our friends in every land and will enable us to march in the vanguard of the United Nations in majestic enjoyment of our fame and power.

—Election broadcast, London, June 30, 1945

The decision of the British people has been recorded in the votes counted today. I have therefore laid down the charge which was placed upon me in darker times. I regret that I have not been permitted to finish the work against Japan. . . . It only remains for me to express to the British people, for whom I have acted in these perilous years, my profound gratitude for the unflinching, unswerving support which they have given me during my task, and for the many expressions of kindness which they have shown towards their servant.

—Upon his resignation as prime minister,
No. 10 Downing Street, July 26, 1945

Let no man underrate the abiding power of the British Empire and Commonwealth. Because you see the 46 millions in our island harassed about their food supply, of which they only grow one half, even in wartime, or because we have difficulty in restarting our industries and export trade after six years of passionate war effort, do not suppose that we shall not come through these dark years of privation as we have come through the glorious years of agony, or that half a century from now, you will not see 70 or 80 millions of Britons spread about the world and united in defense of our traditions, our way of life, and of the world causes which you and we espouse.

—Address at Westminster College, Fulton, Missouri, March 5, 1946

In a long and varied life I have constantly watched and tried to measure the moods and inspirations of the British people. There is no foe they will not face. There is no hardship they cannot endure. Whether the test be sharp and short or long and wearisome, they can take it. What they do not forgive is false promises and vain boastings.

—Remarks on October 4, 1947

The Island is beset by a tribe of neurotic philosophers who, on awakening, begin each day by thinking what there is of Britain that they can give away, and end each day by regretting what they have done.

—Commenting on the Labor government, August 9, 1947

"All men are created equal," says the American Declaration of Independence. "All men shall be kept equal," says the British Socialist Party.

—Election address at Huddersfield, England, October 15, 1951

I, whose youth was passed in the august, unchallenged and tranquil glories of the Victorian Era, may well feel a thrill in invoking, once more, the prayer and the Anthem, "God Save the Queen!"

—Broadcast, London, February 7, 1952

AMERICA

What an extraordinary people the Americans are! Their hospitality is a revelation to me and they make you feel at home and at ease in a way that I have never before experienced.

—Letter to his brother Jack during his first visit to America in 1895,
Churchill in America, 1895–1961: An Affectionate Portrait by Robert H. Pilpel

My lecture tour in the States has been fully booked up, and the Agency have had no difficulty in letting the largest halls at the highest prices.

—Letter to Bernard Baruch, 1931,
Churchill in America, 1895–1961: An Affectionate Portrait by Robert H. Pilpel

Whatever the pathway of the future may bring, we can face it more safely, more comfortably, and more happily if we travel it together, like good companions. We have quarreled in the past, but even in our quarrels great leaders on both sides were agreed on principle. Let our common tongue, our common basic law, our joint heritage of literature and ideals, the red tie of kinship, become the sponge of obliteration of all the unpleasantness of the past.

—Speech in Atlanta, February 23, 1932

Meeting Roosevelt was like uncorking your first bottle of Champagne.

—Remarks on his relationship with Roosevelt, from PBS series
American Experience, "The Presidents: FDR"

I wish to be Prime Minister and in close and daily communication by telephone with the President of the United States. There is nothing we could not do if we were together.

—Remarks on October 8, 1933

The British Empire and the United States will have to be somewhat mixed up together in some of their affairs for mutual and general advantage. For my own part, looking out for the future, I do not view the process with any misgivings. I could not stop it if I wished; no one can stop it. Like the Mississippi, it just keeps rolling along. Let it roll! Let it roll on full flood, inexorable, irresistible, benignant, to broader lands and better days.

—Speech to the House of Commons,
August 20, 1940

I cannot help reflecting that if my father had been American and my mother British instead of the other way around, I might have gotten here on my own.

—Speech to Congress, December 1941

It is fun to be in the same decade with you.

—FDR's cable to Churchill upon FDR's 60th birthday,
January 30, 1942

If we are together nothing is impossible. If we are divided all will fail. I therefore preach continually the doctrine of the fraternal association of our two peoples, not for any purpose of gaining material advantages for either of them, not for territorial aggrandizement or the vain pomp of earthly domination, but for the sake of service to mankind and for the honor that comes to those who faithfully serve great causes.

—Speech at Harvard University, September 6, 1943

The American chiefs do not like to be outdone in generosity. No people respond more spontaneously to fair play. If you treat Americans well they always want to treat you better.

—*The Second World War: The Hinge of Fate,* vol. 4

Twice in my lifetime, the long arm of destiny has reached across the oceans and involved the entire life and manhood of the United States in a deadly struggle. There was no use in saying: "We don't want it: we won't have it; our forebears left Europe to avoid these quarrels; we have founded a new world which has no contact with the old." There was no use in that. The long arm reaches out remorselessly, and everyone's existence, environment, and outlook undergo a swift and irresistible change.

—Speech at Harvard University, September 6, 1943

He was the greatest American friend Britain has ever known and the most powerful champion of freedom who has ever brought help and comfort from the new world to the old.

—Radio broadcast in support of British memorial to FDR, November 18, 1946

Great Britain and the United States all one? Yes, I am all for that, and you mean me to run for President?

—Remarks in 1943

I could never run for President of the United States. All that handshaking of people I didn't give a damn about would kill me. Ten minutes here. Ten minutes there. . . . Not for me.

—Remarks circa 1949

At any rate, he is a man of immense determination. He takes no notice of delicate ground, he just plants his foot down firmly upon it.

—On Harry S. Truman, 1945

I have never accepted a position of subservience to the United States. They have welcomed me as the champion of the British point of view. They are a fair-minded people.

—Remarks, October 1951

It cannot be in the interest of Russia to go on irritating the United States. There are no people in the world who are so slow to develop hostile feelings against a foreign country as the Americans, and there are no people who, once estranged, are more difficult to win back.

—Speech to the House of Commons, June 5, 1946

Adlai Stevenson: "What message would you like me to bring from you to the English-Speaking Union?"

Churchill: "My mother was American, my ancestors were officers in Washington's army; so I am myself an English-speaking Union."

—Remarks in 1953

The Prime Minister has nothing to hide from the President of the United States.

—Remarks after stepping from his bath in front of a surprised President Roosevelt, recalled by Roosevelt's son in the BBC television series *Churchill* (1992)

Their national psychology is such that the bigger the Idea the more wholeheartedly and obstinately do they throw themselves into making it a success. It is an admirable characteristic, providing the Idea is good.

—Remarks in 1952

The United States is like a gigantic boiler. Once the fire is lit under it, there is no limit to the power it can generate. . . . I am, as you know, half American by blood, and the story of my association with that mighty and benevolent nation goes back nearly ninety years to the day of my Father's marriage. In this century of storm and tragedy I contemplate with high satisfaction the constant factor of the interwoven and upward progress of our peoples. Our comradeship and our brotherhood in war were unexampled. We stood together, and because of that fact the free world now stands. Nor has our partnership any exclusive nature: the Atlantic community is a dream that can well be fulfilled to the detriment of none and to the enduring benefit and honor of the great democracies.

—From the written statement in response to his being made
an honorary U.S. citizen by President John F. Kennedy

The whole history of this country shows a British instinct—and I think I may say, a genius—for the division of power. The American constitution, with its checks and counter checks, combined with its frequent appeals to the people, embodied much of the ancient wisdom of this island.

—Remarks, November 11, 1947

RUSSIA

Lenin was sent into Russia by the Germans in the same way that you might send a phial containing a culture of typhoid or cholera to be poured into the water supply of a great city, and it worked with amazing accuracy.

—Speech to the House of Commons,
November 1919

There is not one single social or economic principle or concept in the philosophy of the Russian Bolshevik which has not been realized, carried into action, and enshrined in immutable laws a million years ago by the white ant.

—Remarks in 1927

I cannot forecast to you the action of Russia. It is a riddle wrapped in a mystery inside an enigma.

—First war-time broadcast as First Lord of the Admiralty,
October 1, 1939

Everybody has always underrated the Russians. They keep their own secrets alike from foe and friends.

—Remarks in 1942

Trying to maintain good relations with a Communist is like wooing a crocodile. You do not know whether to tickle it under the chin or beat it over the head. When it opens its mouth, you cannot tell whether it is trying to smile or preparing to eat you up.

—Remarks in 1944

I deem it highly important that we shake hands with the Russians as far east as possible.

—Message to Eisenhower, 1945

From what I have seen of our Russian friends and allies during the war I am convinced that there is nothing they admire so much as strength and nothing for which they have less respect than weakness—particularly military weakness.

—Address, Westminster College, Fulton, Missouri,
March 5, 1946

From Stettin in the Baltic to Trieste in the Adriatic an iron curtain has descended across the Continent.

—Speech at Westminster College, Fulton, Missouri,
March 5, 1946

What we are faced with is not a violent jerk but a prolonged pull.

—Remarks on the Cold War, House of Commons,
March 1953

HISTORY

The whole history of the world is summed up in the fact that when nations are strong they are not always just, and when they wish to be just, they are often no longer strong.

—Speech to the House of Commons, March 26, 1936

History with its flickering lamp stumbles along the trail of the past, trying to reconstruct its scenes, to revive its echoes, and kindle with pale gleams the passion of former days.

—Speech to the House of Commons, November 12, 1940

Persevere towards those objectives which are lighted for us by all the wisdom and inspiration of the past.

—Remarks in 1948

If we open a quarrel between the past and present, we shall find we have lost the future.

—Speech to the House of Commons, June 18, 1940

For my part, I consider that it will be found much better by all parties to leave the past to history, especially as I propose to write that history myself.

—Speech to the House of Commons, January 23, 1948

At times of crisis, myths have their historical importance.

—To Bill Deakin, his literary assistant, about
A History of the English-Speaking Peoples

We cannot undo the past, but we are bound to pass it in review in order to draw from it such lessons as may be applicable to the future. . . .

—Remarks in 1936

As history unfolds itself, by strange and unpredictable paths, we have little control over the future and no control at all over the past.

—Speech at the Society of Cincinnati,
Washington, D.C., January 16, 1952

How strange it is that the past is so little understood and so quickly forgotten. We live in the most thoughtless of ages. Every day headlines and short views. I have tried to drag history up a little nearer to our own times in case it should be helpful as a guide in present difficulties.

—Remarks on April 5, 1929

PEACE, WAR, THE MILITARY, AND FOREIGN POLICY

Peace will not be preserved by pious sentiments. It will not be preserved by casting aside in dangerous times the panoply of warlike strength.

. . . Moralists may find it a melancholy thought that peace can find no nobler foundation than mutual terror.

—Speech to the House of Commons, March 5, 1952

How many wars have been avoided by patience and good will?

. . . No one can guarantee success in war, but only deserve it.

. . . It is a shame that war should have flung all this aside in its greedy, base, opportunistic march, and should turn instead to chemists in spectacles and chauffeurs pulling levers of airplanes or machine guns.

—Remarks in 1898, reflecting on the cavalry charge at Omdurman

Keep cool, men! This will be interesting for my paper!

—Remarks to soldiers at the Boer ambush of an armored train on which he was riding as a war correspondent for the *Morning Post*, 1899

Nothing in life is so exhilarating as to be shot at without result.

—*The Story of the Malakand Field Force*

This kind of war was full of fascinating thrills. It was not like the Great War. Nobody expected to be killed. Here and there in every regiment or battalion, half a dozen, a score, at the worst thirty or forty, would pay the forfeit; but to the great mass of those who took part in the little wars of Britain in those vanished light-hearted days, this was only a sporting element in a splendid game.

—Referring to the Battle of Omdurman,
from *My Early Life: A Roving Commission*

The bullet is brutally indiscriminating, and before it the brain of a hero or the quarters of a horse stand exactly the same chance to the vertical square inch.

—Remarks in 1899

I think a curse should rest on me—because I love this war. I know it's smashing and shattering the lives of thousands every moment—and yet—I can't help it—I enjoy every second of it.

—From a letter to a friend, 1916

No one can tell how far this great adventure may carry us all. Unless we win, I do not want to live any more. But win we will.

—Letter to his brother Jack, August 24, 1914

Before the war it had seemed incredible that such terrors and slaughters, even if they began, could last more than a few months. After the first two years it was difficult to believe that they would ever end. We seemed separated from the old life by a measureless gulf.

. . . The Great War differed from all ancient wars in the immense power of the combatants and their fearful agencies of destruction, and from all modern wars in the utter ruthlessness with which it was fought.

—*The World Crisis*

War attracts me and fascinates my mind with its tremendous situations. What vile and wicked folly and barbarism it all is.

—Remarks in 1903

There have been many occasions when a powerful state has wished to raise great armies, and with money and time and discipline and loyalty that can be accomplished. Nevertheless the rate at which the small American Army of only a few hundred thousand men, not long before the war, created the mighty force of millions of soldiers, is a wonder in military history.

—Speech at the Pentagon, March 9, 1946

I have always urged fighting wars and other contentions with might and main till overwhelming victory, and then offering the hand of friendship to the vanquished. Thus I have always been against the Pacifists during the quarrel, and against the Jingoes at its close.

. . . In wartime, truth is so precious that she should always be attended by a bodyguard of lies.

—Remarks in 1943, referring to Stalin's approval of fake invasion plans for the 1944 invasion of France

There is only one thing worse than fighting with allies, and that is fighting without them.

—Frequent remark

In working with allies it sometimes happens that they develop opinions of their own.

—Remarks in 1942

The Dark Ages may return—the Stone Age may return on the gleaming wings of science; and what might now shower immeasurable material blessings upon mankind may even bring about its total destruction. Beware, I say! Time may be short.

—Referring to nuclear war

One of my fundamental ideas has always been the importance of keeping as many options as possible open to serve the main purpose, especially in time of war.

. . . Nobody keeps armaments going for fun. They keep them going for fear.

—Remarks on November 23, 1945

To try to be safe everywhere is to be strong nowhere.

—Remarks in 1951

Hope flies on wings, and international conferences plod afterwards along dusty roads.

—Remarks on January 7, 1925, at a conference
of finance ministers in Paris

The reason for having diplomatic relations is not to confer a compliment, but to secure a convenience.

—Remarks in 1949

FAMILY AND FRIENDS

Where does a family start? It starts with a young man falling in love with a girl—no superior alternative has yet been found.

—Speech to the House of Commons, November 6, 1950

There is no doubt that it is around the family and the home that all the greatest virtues, the most dominating virtues of human society, are created, strengthened and maintained.

—Remarks upon the birth of Prince Charles, 1948

The whole theme of motherhood and family life, with those sweet affections which illuminate it, must be the fountain spring of present happiness and future survival.

. . . The wine of life was in her veins. Sorrows and storms were conquered by her nature and on the whole it was a life of sunshine.

—To Lord Curzon upon the death of Churchill's mother, 1921,
Churchill: A Life by Martin Gilbert

There are no words to convey to you the feelings of love & joy by wh[ich] my being is possessed. May God who has given me so much more than I ever knew how to ask keep you safe and sound.

—Letter to Clementine shortly after their engagement,
Clementine Churchill: The Biography of a Marriage by Mary Soames

Most people grow tired before they are over-tired. But Lord Randolph was of the temper that gallops until it falls.

—*Lord Randolph Churchill*

Lord Randolph Churchill's place in our political history is measured not by his words and actions, but by the impression which his personality made upon his contemporaries. This was intense, and had circumstances continued favorable, might well have manifested itself in decisive episodes. He embodied that force, caprice and charm which so often springs from genius. . . . More than ever do I regret that we did not live long enough in company to know each other.

—*My Early Life: A Roving Commission*

I am not rich nor powerfully established, but your daughter loves me & with that love I feel strong enough to assume this great & sacred responsibility; & I think I can make her happy & give her a station & career worthy of her beauty and her virtues.

—Letter to Lady Blanch Hozier upon his engagement to Clementine, 1908, *Churchill: A Life* by Martin Gilbert

Oh my darling do not write of "friendship" to me—I love you more each month that passes and feel the need of you & all your beauty. . . . I am so devoured of egoism that I would like to have another soul in another world & meet you in another setting, & pay you all the love & honor of the great romances.

—Letter to Clementine from the trenches in France during World War I, 1916,
Churchill: A Life by Martin Gilbert

My darling one,
This is only to give you
my fondest love and kisses
a hundred times repeated.
I am a pretty dull and
paltry scribbler; but my
stick as it writes carries my
heart along with it.
Your ever & always
W.

—Letter to Clementine from 88-year-old Winston,
Churchill: A Life by Martin Gilbert

What do they need?—cigars, Champagne and a double bed.

—Remark in 1939 about the marriage of his son Randolph to
Pamela Digby, which occurred within weeks of their engagement

His generosity was as much in evidence as his temper, his humor, and his tears. He ordered that the Chartwell gates remain open as a sign of welcome to any neighbors who might be inclined to stop by. Many did.

—William Manchester and Paul Reid,
The Last Lion: Defender of the Realm, 1940–1965

It is splendid having you at home to think about me & love me & share my inmost fancies. What shd I find to hold on to without you. All my gt political estate seems to have vanished away—all my friends are mute—all my own moyens are in abeyance. But there is the Kat with her kittens, supplied I trust adequately with cream & occasional mice. That is all my world in England. . . .

—Letter to Clementine from France, 1915,
Clementine Churchill: The Biography of a Marriage by Mary Soames

What you say is very grandfatherly. You're always giving me grandfatherly advice. You're not my grandfather, you know.

—To his son Randolph, 1945,
The Definitive Wit of Winston Churchill edited by Richard M. Langworth

Winston was more relaxed and indulgent, greatly enjoying his children in the brief moments he could spend with them. His letters show a touching interest and concern for his nursery. His children, and later his grandchildren, were always conscious that he loved to have them around.

—Mary Soames, the youngest of the Churchill children, from
Clementine Churchill: The Biography of a Marriage by Mary Soames

The most precious thing I have in life is yr love for me. I reproach myself for many shortcomings. You are a rock & I depend on you & rest on you. . . .

—Letter to Clementine, March 1925,
Clementine Churchill: The Biography of a Marriage by Mary Soames

Copyright 1900.
by
J. E. Purdy.
Boston.
-2-

LIFE'S PLEASURES

I soon experienced a real pleasure in the task of writing, and the three or four hours in the middle of every day, often devoted to slumber or cards, saw me industriously at work.

—Referring in *My Early Life: A Roving Commission*,
to his first book, *The Malakand Field Force*

To sit at one's table on a sunny morning, with four clear hours of uninterruptible security, plenty of nice white paper, and a Squeezer pen [newly invented type of fountain pen]—that is true happiness.

—Speech at the Author's Club, London, February 17, 1908

If you cannot read all your books, at any rate handle, or as it were, fondle them—peer into them, let them fall open where they will, read from the first sentence that arrests the eye, set them back on their shelves with your own hands, arrange them on your own plan so that if you do not know what is in them, you at least know where they are. Let them be your friends, let them at any rate be your acquaintances.

—*Sir Winston Churchill: His Life and His Paintings*
by David Coombs with Minnie Churchill

Writing a book is an adventure. To begin with it is a toy, then an amusement. Then it becomes a mistress, and then it becomes a master, and then it becomes a tyrant and, in the last stage, just as you are about to be reconciled to your servitude, you kill the monster, and fling him to the public.

—Remarks in November 1949

How I wish you could be there. It really is a delightful valley and the garden gleams with summer jewelry. We live very simply—but with all the essentials of life well understood and provided for—hot baths, cold Champagne, new peas & old brandy.

—Letter to his brother Jack, who was serving at Gallipoli, referring to Hoe Farm, his cottage in Surrey where Churchill and his family took refuge after his disgraced departure from the admiralty in 1915, *Churchill Style: The Art of Being Winston Churchill* by Barry Singer

Painting is a friend, who makes no undue demands, excites to no exhausting pursuits, keeps faithful pace even with feeble steps and holds her canvas as a screen between us and the envious eyes of time or the surly advance of Decrepitude.

—Quoted in *Sir Winston Churchill: His Life and His Paintings* by David Coombs with Minnie Churchill

I prefer landscapes. A tree doesn't complain that I haven't done it justice.

—In response to a friend's question about why he painted landscapes, circa 1930s

I cannot pretend to feel impartial about the colors. I rejoice with the brilliant ones, and am genuinely sorry for the poor browns. When I get to heaven I mean to spend a considerable portion of my first million years in painting, and so get to the bottom of the subject.

—Interview in the *Strand* Magazine,
December 1921–January 1922

A remarkable example of modern art. It certainly combines force and candor.

—Remarks upon his 80th birthday, on the much-anticipated portrait of
Churchill by Graham Sutherland, *Churchill: A Life* by Martin Gilbert. The
portrait, despised by Churchill, was later burned by Lady Churchill

We shape our buildings, and afterwards our buildings shape us. Having dwelt and served for more than forty years in the late Chamber, and having derived very great pleasure and advantage therefrom, I, naturally, should like to see it restored in all essentials to its old form, convenience and dignity.

—Speech to the House of Commons (meeting in the House of Lords),
October 28, 1943

Young men have often been ruined through owning horses, or through backing horses, but never through riding them; unless of course they break their necks, which, taken at a gallop, is a very good death to die.

—*My Early Life: A Roving Commission*

Golf is an ineffectual attempt to direct an uncontrollable sphere into an inaccessible hole with instruments ill-adapted to the purpose.

. . . I could not live without Champagne. In victory I deserve it. In defeat I need it.

—To Madame Odette Pol-Roger, 1946

I find alcohol a great support in life. Sir Alexander Walker, who keeps me supplied with your national brew, told me that a friend of his, who died the other day, drank a bottle of whisky a day for the last 10 years of his life. He was 85!

—Letter to Lord Boothby, 1948

Conservation of energy. Never stand up when you can sit down, and never sit down when you can lie down.

—In response to author Paul Johnson's question to Churchill about to what he ascribed his success in life, *Churchill* by Paul Johnson

I must point out that my rule of life prescribes as an absolutely sacred rite smoking cigars and also the drinking of alcohol before, after, and if the need be during all meals and in the intervals between them.

. . . How can I tell that the soothing influence of tobacco upon my nervous system may not have enabled me to comport myself with calm and with courtesy in some awkward personal encounter or negotiation, or carried me serenely through some critical hours of anxious waiting? How can I tell that my temper would have been as sweet or my companionship as agreeable if I had abjured from my youth the goddess Nicotine?

—Remarks in 1931

I get my exercise serving as pall-bearer to my many friends who exercised all their lives.

—Remarks circa 1950

EDUCATION,
KNOWLEDGE,
INFORMATION,
AND INNOVATION

Those who think that we can become richer or more stable as a country by stinting education and crippling the instruction of our young people are a most benighted class of human beings.

—Remarks at Woodford County School for Girls, May 27, 1925

The first duty of the university is to teach wisdom, not a trade; character, not technicalities. We want a lot of engineers in the modern world, but we do not want a world of engineers.

—Speech at University of London, November 18, 1948

Owing to the pressure of life and everyone having to earn their living, a university education of the great majority of those who enjoy that high privilege is usually acquired before twenty. These are great years for young people. The world of thought and history and the treasures of learning are laid open to them. They have the chance of broadening their minds, elevating their view and arming their moral convictions to all the resources that free and wealthy communities can bestow.

—Speech at University of Miami, February 26, 1946

The university education is a guide to the reading of a lifetime. We should impress upon those who have its advantages the importance of reading the great books of the world and the literature of one's own country. One who has profited from university education has a wide choice. He need never be idle or bored and have to take refuge in the clack and clatter of the modern age. . . . There is a good saying, which you have heard before, that when a new book comes out you should read an old one though I perhaps should not recommend too rigid an application.

—Speech at University of London, November 18, 1948

The newspapers do an immense amount of thinking for the average man and woman. In fact they supply them with such a continuous stream of standardized opinion, borne along upon an equally inexhaustible flood of news and sensation, collected from every part of the world every hour of the day, that there is neither the need nor the leisure for personal reflection. All this is but part of a tremendous educating process. But it is an education which passes in at one ear and out at the other. It is an education at once universal and superficial. It produces enormous numbers of standardized citizens, all equipped with regulation opinions, prejudices and sentiments, according to their class or party.

—Essay, "Mass Effects in Modern Life," *Strand Magazine*, 1932

It is a good thing for an uneducated man to read books of quotations. . . . The quotations when engraved upon the memory give you good thoughts. They also make you anxious to read the authors and look for more.

—*My Early Life: A Roving Commission*

I am always ready to learn, although I do not always like being taught.

—Remarks in 1952

If we look back on our past life we shall see that one of its most usual experiences is that we have been helped by our mistakes.

—Remarks in 1931

I do not admire people who are wise after the event. I would rather be impaled on the other horn of the dilemma.

—Remarks in 1935

We want some scientists, but we must keep them in their proper place. Our generation has seen great changes. We have parted company with the horse; we have an internal combustion engine instead and I wonder whether we have gained by the change.

—Speech at the University of London, November 18, 1948

The television has come to take its place in the world; as a rather old-fashioned person I have not been one of its principal champions, but I don't think it needs any champion. I think it can make its own way and I think it's a wonderful thing indeed to think that every expression on my face at this moment may be viewed by millions of people throughout the United States. I hope that the raw material is a good as the methods of distribution.

—Interview on the *Queen Mary* in New York Harbor, 1952,
The Irrepressible Churchill compiled by Kay Halle

We must be aware of needless innovation, especially when guided by logic.

—Remarks in 1942

The empires of the future are the empires of the mind.

—Speech at Harvard University, September 6, 1943

RELIGION, MORALITY, AND VIRTUE

We can find nothing better than Christian ethics on which to build and the more closely we follow the Sermon on the Mount, the more likely we are to succeed in our endeavors.

—Remarks on January 25, 1941

The conflict between good and evil which proceeds unceasingly in the breast of man nowhere reaches such an intensity as in the Jewish race. . . . We owe to the Jews in the Christian revelation a system of ethics which, even if it were entirely separated from the supernatural, would be incomparably the most precious possession of mankind, worth in fact the fruits of all other wisdom and learning put together. On that system and by that faith there has been built out of the wreck of the Roman Empire the whole of our existing civilization.

—Excerpt from "Zionism versus Bolshevism,"
Illustrated Sunday Herald, February 8, 1920

The flame of Christian ethics is still our highest guide. To guard and cherish it is our first interest, both spiritually and materially. The fulfillment of spiritual duty in our daily life is vital to our survival. Only by bringing it into perfect application can we hope to solve for ourselves the problems of this world and not of this world alone.

—Speech at Massachusetts Institute of Technology, March 31, 1949

Only faith in a life after death in a brighter world where dear ones will meet again—only that and the measured tramp of time can give consolation.

—Remarks on September 8, 1942

I deprecate all Romish practices and prefer those of Protestantism . . . . [b]ut at the same time I can see a poor parish—working men living their lives in ugly white-washed factories, toiling day after day amid scenes & surroundings destitute of the element of beauty. I can sympathize with them for their aching longing for something not infected by the general squalor & something to gratify their love of the mystic. . . . I find it hard to rob their lives of this one ennobling aspiration—even though it finds expression in the burning of incense, the wearing of certain robes and other superstitious practices.

—To his cousin Ivor Guest, *Churchill: A Life* by Martin Gilbert

I have made more bishops than anyone since St. Augustine.

—Remarks on August 7, 1942

I am not a pillar of the church but a buttress—I support it from the outside.

—Remarks circa 1954

Except in so far as force is concerned, there is no equality between right and wrong.

—Remarks in 1945

This truth is incontrovertible. Panic may resent it, ignorance may deride it, malice may distort it, but there it is.

—Remarks in 1916

Virtuous motives, trammeled by inertia and timidity, are no match for armed and resolute wickedness.

—Remarks in 1948

I am certainly not one who needs to be prodded. In fact, if anything I am a prod. My difficulties rather lie in finding the patience and self-restraint to wait through many anxious weeks for the results to be achieved.

—Attributed

THE GREAT
COMMUNICATOR

The most durable structures raised in stone by the strength of man, the mightiest monuments of his power, crumble into dust, while the words spoken with fleeting breath, the passing expression of the unstable fancies of his mind, endure not as echoes of the past, not as mere archaeological curiosities or venerable relics, but with a force and life as new and strong, and sometimes far stronger than when they were first spoken, and leaping across the gulf of three thousand years, they light the world for us today.

—Speech addressing audience of authors, 1908

It is this power of words—words written in the past; words spoken at this moment; words printed in the newspapers; words sent speeding through the ether in a Transatlantic broadcast; the flashing interchange of thought—that is our principal agency of union.

—"The Union of the English-Speaking Peoples,"
News of the World, May 15, 1938

If you have an important point to make, don't try to be subtle or clever. Use a pile driver. Hit the point once. Then come back and hit it again. Then hit it a third time.

—Remarks in 1919 to the Prince of Wales, the future Edward VIII

The essence of good House of Commons speaking is the conversational style, the facility for quick, informal interruptions and interchanges. Harangues from a rostrum would be a bad substitute for the conversational style in which so much of our business is done. But the conversational style requires a fairly small space, and there should be on great occasions a sense of crowd and urgency. There should be a sense of the importance of much that is said and a sense that great matters are being decided, there and then, by the House. . . . It has a collective personality which enjoys the regard of the public, and which imposes itself upon the conduct not only of individual Members but of parties.

—Speech in the House of Commons, October 28, 1943

It is pretty tough to reshape human society in an after-dinner speech.

—Response to the draft of a long-winded speech that Halifax, British ambassador in Washington, was proposing to make

Some people's idea of free speech is that they are free to say what they like but if anyone says anything back, that is an outrage.

. . . I have been a journalist and half my lifetime I have earned my living by selling words and, I hope, thoughts.

—Remarks, Ottawa, January 1952

Asking me not to make a speech is like asking a centipede to get along and not put a foot on the ground.

—Remarks in 1940

The English language is the language of the English-speaking people, and no country, or combination or power so fertile and so vivid exists anywhere else on the surface of the globe. We must see that it is not damaged by modern slang, adaptations, or intrusions. We must endeavor to popularize and strengthen our language in every way. Broadly speaking, short words are best, and the old words, when short, are the best of all. Thus, being lovers of English, we will not only improve and preserve our literature, but also make ourselves a more intimate and effective member of the great English-speaking world, on which, if wisely guided, the future of mankind will largely rest.

—Speech upon receiving the London *Times* Literary Award,
November 2, 1949

Of all the talents bestowed upon men, none is so precious as the gift of oratory. He who enjoys it wields a power more durable than that of a great king. He is an independent force in the world. Abandoned by his party, betrayed by his friends, stripped of his offices, whoever can command this power is still formidable.

—Written while stationed in India, 1897, and reiterated
in different versions throughout his life

THE WIT AND
WISDOM OF
WINSTON
CHURCHILL

Usually youth is for freedom and reform, maturity for judicious compromise, and old age for stability and repose.

—Remarks in 1927

I have derived continued benefit from criticism at all periods of my life, and I do not remember any time when I was short of it.

. . . Why should I accept the Order of the Garter from His Majesty, when the people have just given me the order of the boot?

—Speech declining the Order of the Garter from King George VI following Churchill's defeat in the 1945 election

So long as I am acting from duty and conviction, I am indifferent to taunts and jeers. I think they will probably do me more good than harm.

. . . There is all the difference in the world between a man who knocks you down and a man who leaves you alone.

—Remarks in 1944

If Hitler invaded hell I would make at least a favorable reference to the devil in the House of Commons.

—*The Second World War: The Grand Alliance*, vol. 3

Dictators ride to and fro upon tigers from which they dare not dismount. And the tigers are getting hungry.

. . . We are all worms. But I do believe that I am a glow-worm.

—Remarks in 1906

I like pigs. Dogs look up to us. Cats look down on us. Pigs treat us as equals.

. . . The most difficult things for a man to do are to climb a wall leaning towards you, to kiss a girl leaning away from you, and to make an after-dinner speech.

. . . A woman is as old as she looks; a man is as old as he feels; and a boy is as old as he is treated.

—Remarks in 1942, as recalled by President Roosevelt's
companion Daisy Suckley in her diaries

Lady Astor: "If you were my husband, I'd poison your coffee."

Churchill: "If you were my wife, I'd drink it."

—Widely attributed

There is no finer investment for any community than putting milk into babies.

—Radio broadcast, March 21, 1943

Broadly speaking, human beings may be divided into three classes: those who are billed to death, those who are worried to death and those who are bored to death.

—Remarks in 1925

Justice moves slowly and remorselessly upon its path, but it reaches its goal eventually.

—Remarks in 1929

The best evidence of the fairness of any settlement is the fact that it fully satisfies neither party.

—Remarks in 1926

A cavalry charge is very like ordinary life. So long as you are all right, firmly in your saddle, your horse in hand and well armed, lots of enemies will give you wide berth.

. . . No boy or girl should ever be disheartened by lack of success in their youth but should diligently and faithfully continue to persevere and make up for lost time.

We have a lot of anxieties, and one cancels out another very often.

—Remarks in 1943

You must put your head into the lion's mouth if the performance is to be a success.

—Remarks in 1900

The finest combination in the world is power and mercy. The worst combination in the world is weakness and strife.

—Speech to the House of Commons, March 3, 1919

Nature is merciful and does not try her children, man or beast, beyond their compass. It is only when the cruelty of man intervenes that hellish torments appear. For the rest, live dangerously, take things as they come. Fear naught, all will be well.

—Written from hospital after car accident in New York in December 1931
(he'd been hit by a passing car and suffered severe injuries),
Churchill by Paul Johnson

How little can we foresee the consequences either of wise or unwise action, of virtue or of malice! Without this measureless and perpetual uncertainty, the drama of human life would be destroyed.

—Remarks in 1948

All the greatest things are simple, and many can be expressed in a single word: freedom; justice; honor; duty; mercy; hope.

—Speech at United Europe meeting, London, May 14, 1947

What is the use of living, if it be not to strive for noble causes and to make this muddled world a better place for those who will live in it after we are gone? How else can we put ourselves in harmonious relation with the great verities and consolations of the infinite and the eternal? And I avow my faith that we are marching towards better days. Humanity will not be cast down. We are going on swinging bravely forward along the grand high road and already behind the distant mountains is the promise of the sun.

—Speech, Dundee, Scotland, October 10, 1908

We must always be ready to make sacrifices for the great causes; only in that way shall we live to keep our souls alive.

—Remarks in 1948

Tranquility! There is nothing more tranquil than the grave. I will never stifle myself in such a moral and intellectual sepulcher.

—*Sir Winston Churchill: A Self-Portrait*

I have never accepted what many people have kindly said—that I inspired the nation. It was the nation and the race dwelling all round the globe that had the lion's heart. I had the luck to be called upon to give the roar. I also hope that I sometimes suggested to the lion the right place to use his claws.

—Speech to both houses of Parliament in Westminster Hall, upon the celebration of his 80th birthday, November 30, 1954

I am prepared to meet my Maker. Whether my Maker is prepared for the great ordeal of meeting me is another matter.

—Remarks at a news conference in Washington, D.C., 1954, quoted in the *New York Times*, January 25, 1965

I am bored with it all. The journey has been enjoyable and well worth making—once.

—Widely attributed to be Churchill's last words, *Churchill* by Paul Johnson

THE LEGACY OF WINSTON CHURCHILL

[Churchill] was blessed with length of days, and he came to the supreme achievement of his life schooled and disciplined by long experience of great affairs, familiar with the handling and control of national problems, full of practical wisdom, and with a part to play that he alone could most magnificently fill.

—Lord Birkett, British barrister, judge, and politician

In many ways Churchill remained a nineteenth-century man . . . . His valet warmed his brandy snifter over a neatly trimmed candle . . . . He had never ridden a bus.

—William Manchester and Paul Reid, preamble to
The Last Lion: Defender of the Realm, 1940–1965

We meet to honor a man whose honor requires no meeting—for he is the most honored and honorable man to walk the stage of human history in the time in which we live. Whenever and wherever tyranny threatened, he has always championed liberty. Facing firmly toward the future, he has never forgotten the past. Serving six monarchs of his native Great Britain, he has served all men's freedom and dignity. In the dark days and darker nights when Britain stood alone—and most men save Englishmen despaired of England's life—he mobilized the English language and sent it into battle. The incandescent quality of his words illuminated the courage of his countrymen. Given unlimited powers by his citizens, he was ever vigilant to protect their rights. Indifferent himself to danger, he wept over the sorrows of others. A child of the House of Commons, he became in time its father. Accustomed to the hardships of battle, he has no distaste for pleasure. Now his stately Ship of Life, having weathered the severest storms of a troubled century, is anchored in tranquil waters, proof that courage and faith and the zest for freedom are truly indestructible. The record of his triumphant passage will inspire free hearts for all time.

—President John F. Kennedy, Washington, D.C., April 9, 1963, conferring honorary U.S. citizenship to Churchill

His nature, identified with a magnificent enterprise, his countenance, etched by the fires and frosts of great events, had become inadequate to the era of mediocrity.

—Charles de Gaulle, commenting on Churchill's resignation as prime minister in 1945

Winston Churchill led the life that many men would love to live. He survived 50 gunfights and drank 20,000 bottles of Champagne. He won the public schools' fencing cup and rode in the last cavalry charge of the British Army. He created British Petroleum, invented the combat tank, and founded the states of Jordan and Iraq. And of course, by resisting Hitler, he saved Europe and perhaps the world.

—Mark Riebling, "Churchill's Finest Hour," in his review of Paul Johnson's *Churchill*, *City Journal*, vol, 22, no. 4, November 24, 2009

[Churchill was] the last of England's great Victorian statesmen, with views formed when the British lion's roar could silence the world.

—William Manchester, *The Last Lion: Winston Spencer Churchill, Alone: 1932–1940*

———

The world will never truly know, however, just what pals they really were. Roosevelt kept his innermost thoughts to himself and left no written legacy of his views, let alone his deep feelings, toward others. We are better endowed with sources when it comes to Churchill's views of Roosevelt. . . . Churchill no doubt respected Roosevelt because he was president of the United States. He also knew from the moment he assumed leadership of the British government that he must pursue him. But he was exasperated with Roosevelt's delays, back-steps, and obfuscations at a time when Britain was bleeding badly and had no prospect of success alone against Hitler.

—David J. Bercuson and Holger H. Herwig, *One Christmas in Washington: The Secret Meeting Between Roosevelt and Churchill that Changed the World*

———

Nothing impeded Churchill's capacity to inspire his countrymen and to fight for their salvation.

—William Manchester and Paul Reid, preamble to
The Last Lion: Defender of the Realm, 1940–1965

Though 1940 and his wartime years as Prime Minister were, undoubtedly, his glory years, it is my belief that, in terms of moral courage and dogged determination, Winston Churchill's finest hour was in the late 1930s when, reviled by his Party, and denounced as a "war monger," he continued his valiant though vain battle to alert the British people to the impending danger, convinced that united and decisive joint action by the former Allies—Britain, France and the United States— could stop Hitler in his tracks and, even as late as 1936, that it could do so without a shot being fired.

—Winston S. Churchill, Churchill's grandson,
Never Give In!: The Best of Winston Churchill's Speeches

There have been, no doubt, debaters and orators of equal resource and power, but few with that gift of puckish and rather mischievous humor which so endears [Churchill] to us.

—Harold Macmillan, leading Conservative, in speech to the
House of Commons, July 28, 1964

My great-grandfather was a brilliant man. His leadership skills, his quotes, his service to his country continue to be a hot topic even today. Most any time you turn on the television, you will hear someone quoting my great-grandfather. But what a lot of people do not know, is that he had a wicked sense of humor and was also an artist.

—Jonathan Churchill Sandy, Churchill's great-grandson,
quoted in an article by Rebecca Maitland
for the Historic Richmond Association

Ultimately, of course, it was not Churchill's Britain alone that broke Germany's back and laid Hitler low. She was not strong enough for that; for that she needed an alliance with the two giants, America and Russia. Nonetheless, had it not been for Britain's grim determination while standing alone between June 1940 and June 1941, that highly incongruous alliance might never have come about. Moreover, without Churchill, Britain might not have been so grimly determined.

—Sebastian Haffner, *Churchill*
(translated by John Brownjohn)

Winston Churchill may have had a lust for war, but we may also be grateful that there was one politician in the 1930s who found it intolerable even to breathe the same air, or share the same continent or planet, as the Nazis.

—Christopher Hitchens,
Newsweek, June 14, 2008

Although a born fighter, Churchill was humane to the point of soft-heartedness, rather in the way that many enthusiastic hunters of game are great animal lovers. He detested the infliction of cruelty on the weak and defeated, and that form of cruelty was, of course, one of Hitler's most salient characteristics. But to believe that purely personal feelings of hatred were Churchill's motive for waging a world war would be to underestimate him. Besides, it is remarkable how his hatred of Hitler waned in the course of the war. The tone in which he spoke of him in public changed. Abuse and unbridled vituperation were gradually replaced by mockery until in 1945, the year of the victory, Churchill ceased to refer to Hitler at all. Hitler no longer interested him.

—Sebastian Haffner, *Churchill*
(translated by John Brownjohn)

No man did more to preserve freedom and democracy and the values we hold dear in the West. None provided more public entertainment with his dramatic ups and downs, his noble oratory, his powerful writings and sayings, his flashes of rage, and his sunbeams of wit. He took a prominent place on the public stage of his country and the world for over sixty years, and it seemed empty with his departure. Nor has anyone since combined so felicitously such a powerful variety of roles.

—Paul Johnson, *Churchill*

As the years pass and the historical record is studied without malice, Churchill's actions and aims will be seen to have been humane and far-sighted. His patriotism, his sense of fair play, his belief in democracy, and his hopes for the human race, were matched by formidable powers of work and thought, vision and foresight. His path was often beset by controversy, disappointment and abuse, but these never deflected him from his sense of duty and his faith in the British people.

—Martin Gilbert,
Churchill: A Life

I now put Churchill, with all his idiosyncrasies, his indulgences, his occasional childishness, but also his genius, his tenacity and his persistent ability, right or wrong, successful or unsuccessful, to be larger than life, as the greatest human being to occupy 10 Downing Street.

—Roy Jenkins,
Churchill: A Biography

The day may dawn when fair play, love for one's fellow men, respect for justice and freedom, will enable tormented generations to march forth serene and triumphant from the hideous epoch in which we have to dwell. Meanwhile, never flinch, never weary, never despair.

—Churchill's last speech to the the House of Commons,
March 1, 1955

CHRONOLOGY

CHRONOLOGY

November 30, 1874 — Winston Leonard Spencer Churchill is born prematurely at Blenheim Palace, Oxfordshire, England. He is the son of Lord Randolph Churchill, the younger son of the 7th Duke of Marlborough, and Jennie Jerome Churchill, daughter of Leonard Jerome, an American stockbroker and part owner of the *New York Times.*

1880 — Winston's brother John Strange Churchill "Jack" is born.

1881 to 1892 — Attends school at Ascot, Brighton, and Harrow.

1893 — Enters Royal Military College, Sandhurst, as a cavalry cadet, after two failed attempts.

1894 — Commissioned a cavalry subaltern, Fourth Hussars.

1895 — Lord Randolph Churchill dies; WSC's beloved nanny, Mrs. Everett dies; makes first visit to United States; acts as war correspondent in Cuba.

1896 — Left for India with the 4th Queen's Own Hussars as a second lieutenant; embarks on regimen of self-education through reading. Discovers historians Macaulay and Gibbon.

1897 — Joins the Malakand Field Force on the Northwest Frontier; sends dispatches to the *Daily Telegraph.*

1898 — Participates in Sudan expedition; writes dispatches for London *Morning Post*; publishes his first book, *The Story of the Malakand Field Force*; participates in Battle of Omdurman; leaves for India to rejoin his regiment.

1899 — Leaves army for career in politics; makes an unsuccessful run for Parliament as a Conservative; acts as war correspondent for the *Morning Post* in Boer War; two weeks after his arrival, he is captured by the Boers. He escapes from Pretoria into Portuguese East Africa and then to Durban; publishes *The River War.*

1900 — Publishes *Savrola*; *London to Ladysmith via Pretoria*; and *Ian Hamilton's March*. He is elected Conservative member of Parliament. Begins a lecture tour in New York City; meets Theodore Roosevelt, the vice-president elect, in Albany.

1901 — Takes his seat in Parliament.

1904 — Abandons the Conservatives in favor of the Liberal Party.

1906 — Publishes *Lord Randolph Churchill*. Elected Liberal member of Parliament; named under-secretary of state for the Colonies.

1907 — Tours East Africa as under-secretary for the Colonies.

1908 — Publishes *My African Journey*. Elected president of the Board of Trade. Elected member of Parliament to represent Dundee. Marries Clementine Hozier.

1909 — First child, Diana, is born; publishes *Liberalism and the Social Problem*.

1910 — Publishes *The People's Rights*; reelected Liberal member for Dundee; appointed home secretary.

1911 — Birth of only son, Randolph. Becomes first lord of the admiralty.

1912 — Instructs naval engineers to devise what would become the first tanks.

1912 to 1914 — Irish Home Rule crisis.

1913 — Learns to fly and establishes the Royal Navy Flying Corps.

1914 — Outbreak of World War I. Birth of second daughter, Sarah.

1915 — The Dardanelles failure. Churchill is deemed responsible and resigns as first lord of the admiralty. Appointed chancellor of the Duchy of Lancaster, resigns from cabinet to join army in France. Commissioned and sent to the front; commands 6th battalion, The Royal Scots Fusiliers.

1916 — Returns to House of Commons.

1917 — Named minister of munitions.

1918 — World War I ends; birth of third daughter, Marigold. Becomes secretary of state for war and minister for air.

1919 — Peace Treaty signed at Versailles; becomes chief supporter of anti-Bolsheviks.

1921 — Becomes colonial secretary. Supports Jewish homeland. Lady Randolph Churchill dies in London. Daughter Marigold dies. Helps to found Irish Free State.

1922 — Fourth daughter, Mary, is born.

1922 to 1924 — Loses three elections; Leaves Liberal Party to rejoin the Conservatives; wins seat in the general election. Becomes chancellor of the exchequer. Publishes *The World Crisis*, volume I (six volumes between 1921–1931).

1924 — Rejoins Conservative Party. Warns of the dangers posed by Germany.

1925 — Returns Great Britain to the gold standard.

1927 — Visits Mussolini in Rome.

1929 — Tours the United States. Loses small fortune in stock market crash.

1930 — Publishes *My Early Life: A Roving Commission*.

1931 — Quits Tory government over India question. Leaves for a lecture tour in New York; is hit by a car and suffers severe injuries. Publishes *India*.

1932 — Resumes U.S. lecture tour. FDR elected U.S. president. Publishes *Amid These Storms*.

1933 — Publishes first of four volumes of *Marlborough: His Life and Times* (1933–1938). Hitler seizes power in Germany.

1934 — Gives first major speech on air defense.

1935 — Hitler disavows Versailles, signs naval treaty with Britain, and enacts anti-Semitic laws. Mussolini invades Ethiopia.

1936 — King George V dies. Hitler takes over Rhineland. King Edward VIII abdicates. Hitler and Mussolini form Axis.

1937 — Coronation of King George VI. Publishes *Great Contemporaries*.

1938 — Anthony Eden quits as foreign secretary. Hitler seizes power in Austria. WSC proposes alliance to defeat Hitler; Chamberlain rejects. Munich Agreement results in partition of portions of Czechoslovakia to Germany. Publishes *Arms and the Covenant* (titled *Why England Slept* in U.S.)

1939 — Publishes *Step by Step*. Defeats appeasers' attempts to oust him. Hitler seizes all of Czechoslovakia and enters Prague. Mussolini invades Albania. German-Soviet Non-Aggression Pact signed. Hitler invades Poland. WSC becomes again the first lord of the admiralty and Britain and France declare war on Germany. Italy remains neutral. Russia invades Finland.

1940 — Finns surrender to Russians. Nazis invades Denmark and Norway, followed by France, Luxembourg, Holland, and Belgium. Neville Chamberlain resigns and WSC becomes prime minister. France and Holland surrender. Dunkirk evacuation. Italy declares war. Belgium surrenders. Latvia, Estonia, and Lithuania are invaded by Soviet Union. WSC orders destruction of French fleet at Oran. Battle of Britain begins.

1941 — Germany invades Russia; WSC promises aid. Japan attacks Pearl Harbor. First wartime meeting with FDR. U.S. enters the war.

1944 — Visits Normandy beaches four days after D-Day. Liberation of Paris.

1945 — Meets with FDR at Malta; and with FDR and Stalin at Yalta. FDR dies.

May 8, 1945 — V-E Day and unconditional surrender of Nazis. Meets at Potsdam with Truman and decides jointly to use atomic bomb against Japan. Defeated in general election, resigns as prime minister, and is succeeded by Clement Atlee. Atomic bombs dropped on Japan.

August 14, 1945 — V-J Day, Japan surrenders.

1946 — Gives historic "iron curtain" speech at Fulton, Missouri. Publishes *Victory*; publishes *Secret Session Speeches*.

1948 — Publishes first of four volumes of *The Second World War*. King George VI relinquishes title of Emperor of India. Harry S. Truman elected his own term as U.S. president. Republic of Ireland bill passed. WSC publishes *Painting as a Pastime*.

1951 — Publishes *In the Balance*. WSC becomes prime minister for second time following Conservative victory.

1952 — General Eisenhower elected U.S. president.

1953 — Awarded Nobel Prize for Literature. WSC knighted by Queen Elizabeth II.

1955 — WSC resigns and is succeeded by Anthony Eden as prime minister.

1956 — Publishes *A History of the English-Speaking Peoples* (1956–1958).

1961 — Publishes *The Unwritten Alliance*.

1963 — President Kennedy honors Churchill with U.S. citizenship; he thus becomes the first honorary U.S. citizen.

1964 — Retires from politics.

January 24, 1965 — Winston Churchill dies at home in London at the age of 90 after suffering a stroke earlier in the month. He dies on the 70th anniversary of the death of his father, Lord Randolph Churchill.

January 30, 1965 — State funeral of Winston Churchill is held.